The World of
DOGS

The World of
DOGS

Angela Sayer

Optimum Books

Photographic acknowledgments
Bruce Coleman–B & C Calhoun 7 top; Bruce Coleman–Hans
Reinhard 7 bottom; Colour Library International front and
back covers; Sally Anne Thompson, Animal Photography
endpapers, frontispiece, 11 top, 11 bottom, 14, 18, 32, 34 top,
34 bottom, 35 top, 36 top, 36 bottom, 37, 39 top,
39 bottom, 41 top, 44, 45 bottom, 46 top, 48 bottom.
All other photographs by Angela Sayer.

This edition published by Optimum Books 1982

Prepared by
The Hamlyn Publishing Group Limited
London·New York·Sydney·Toronto
Astronaut House, Feltham, Middlesex, England

Copyright © The Hamlyn Publishing Group Limited 1982
ISBN 0 600 37868 3

Printed in Italy

Contents

The Dog and Man

In fossil terms the evolution of the dog is a fairly recent occurrence for modern man's most popular pet left traces of its first domesticated form in the deposits of only 12000 years ago. Such early canine discoveries have been made in northern Israel and in a cave in Iraq. Slightly more recent fossilized dogs have been discovered as far apart as Idaho in the United States of America and Staw Cave in Yorkshire, England, as well as Switzerland, Denmark and Turkey, and have been dated from 8000 to 10500 years ago.

The earlier history of the dog, before the days of its domestication, probably began some time between the Eocene and Oligocene periods of about 40 mil-

lion years ago, a time when the great land masses grew at the expense of the seas. The Earth enjoyed generally warm, temperate conditions and the increase in grass-eating mammals led to the evolution of carnivores. From *Miacis*, a small, tenacious forest-dweller, came three groups of descendants: the ancestors of the seals, walruses and other finned animals; the ancestors of the cats, civets and their cousins; and the ancestors of the dogs and related species.

The remains of the earliest true dog, *Hesperocyon*, found in Oligocene deposits in North America, show the animal to be small, resembling a desert fox with some characteristics of its *miacid* forebears. *Cynodictis*, another primitive dog,

A feral dog acting as a self-appointed guardian of a ruined Egyptian temple.

6

Left: The modern wolf is very similar to the wolf-like ancestors of today's dogs.

Below: Even our domesticated canine pets retain the primitive instincts and responses of their fierce wild forebears.

was common in the Lower Oligocene, and had achieved the size of a fox. It had five-toed feet and probably possessed retractile claws. Gradually larger dogs evolved with characteristics more suited to hunting on open plains than stalking in the forests.

Canis familiaris, our domestic dog, is the cause of much controversy among scientists, who disagree about its direct ancestors. The general concensus of opinion today, however, favours the theory that four quite different families of wolves have given rise to the forebears of all the diverse dog breeds of today. The modern dogs may be grouped as follows: the Spitz varieties, Collies and Terriers have descended from the Northern Grey Wolf; the Dingo group comes from the Pale-footed Asian Wolf; a long-legged relative of the Asian Wolf produced the dogs of the Greyhound type; and all the Mastiffs, Gundogs and Hounds probably descended from the Wooly-coated Wolves from China and Tibet.

It is thought that dogs were originally used by man as natural allies in hunting. As both aimed to kill the same prey and came to realize the futility of working against each other, they soon found that a distant but cooperative relationship was beneficial to both groups. Both man

7

and wolf or dog worked in packs or groups, and shared similar social systems based on family units.

Another theory behind domestication suggests that young wolf cubs, captured during hunting, were brought back to the human encampments and reared as pets. While it may be difficult to accept this, bearing in mind how much hard-earned food would be necessary to rear such a non-productive animal, support has been given by an interesting fossil find in Israel. The skeleton of a puppy was excavated, a human hand resting protectively upon it, and suggests that companionship between dog and man was established at the date of the deposits, some 12 000 years ago. If this theory is correct, then it may be argued that the working potential of the dog was exploited after it had become the trusted friend of man.

Yet another theory suggests that man first adopted the dog for its guarding behaviour. Its superior senses of sight and smell alerted all to any threat of danger.

Finally it has been suggested that the dog's domestication happened almost casually, with the relationship developing on a mutual basis, while both were hunting similar prey. Man used the wolves' tracking abilities to corner and catch animals for his own group, and the wolves hung around the campsite picking up all the discarded scraps.

No one will ever know the true story of the domestication of the dog, but it is good to know that we may each believe in our own favourite theories of how we first came to terms with him.

Domestication was certainly successful and man soon began to develop dogs by selectively breeding for desired traits.

The PHARAOH HOUND, *Olio Amenophis of Edgeelmclere*, shows a remarkable resemblance to hounds found etched in reliefs of Ancient Egypt.

There are cave paintings in the Pyrenees dating from Paleolithic times which clearly show archers and wolf-like dogs working together in a hunting scene.

In Britain in 1928 the excavation of a Neolithic settlement commenced. Situated at Avebury in Wiltshire, the now-famous Windmill Hill dog was discovered which showed that as long ago as 2500 B.C. domesticated dogs were bred to have certain characteristics and were far removed from their wolf ancestors. Although the Windmill Hill dog's location and attitude gave no clue as to its precise function in the ancient settlement, its remains show a well-developed jaw and powerful shoulders, so the animal was adapted for holding firmly to its prey, and points to it being a hunting dog or guard, although it was small in stature.

In contrast the huge mastiff-like dogs, represented in Babylonian art of about the same period, were probably used as dogs of war, and those of the Ancient Egyptians, long-legged and sleek, were the forebears of our sight hounds. Thus we can see that even several thousand years ago, man had used his powers of selection to develop several different groups of dogs, suitable for quite different purposes and far removed in appearance from their wild ancestors.

As well as breeding dogs for war, guarding and herding, dogs were developed for hunting certain game. Packs of hounds which hunted by scent were found particularly useful for tracking some types of game, while in open country sight hounds were more efficient. Small fierce dogs were required to hunt below ground, flushing out their prey from burrows and lairs. In all cases the dogs had to be taught that the prey was for their masters, not to be devoured.

Natural protective instincts produced both guarding and herding dogs, and some breeds, even today, excel in both related respects. The dog's natural degree of adaptiveness appealed to man and every newly noticed trait was exploited. Eventually man became slightly more prosperous and he began to keep dogs for non-utilitarian purposes. He had become a breeder and could manipulate his animals' characteristics to suit his own purposes. He began to keep dogs for their appearance

and temperament rather than their skills, and the pet dog was born.

Well-to-do ladies kept small dogs which they called 'comforters'. These were pet dogs which spent the larger part of the day sitting on their mistresses' laps. They were favoured for relieving mild abdominal pains by the warmth of their bodies, and attracted lice and fleas from their owners' persons onto their own skin, from which they were carefully picked and killed.

Joe Kapelos carefully trains his RED MERLE AUSTRALIAN SHEPHERD *Big Maple Tonya*.

Right: In the frozen Arctic wastes, sled dogs such as this one are invaluable workers.

Below: Trained to perfection, the guide dog leads its blind handler safely across the road.

Some peoples relied heavily on their dogs in order to survive, and in some regions this is still the case. In the Arctic a number of distinct types of sled dogs were developed, the purity of their lines being protected solely by the isolated situation of their settlements. Such dogs were carefully reared and used for haulage during their prime, then they were killed and used for food and their skins used for clothing. Their places in the teams were taken over by young, newly trained adults.

Hunting dogs have always been necessary to the survival of many peoples of the world, easily earning their own keep by helping to keep the cooking pots well filled. Such dogs are also used today for sporting purposes, either tracking down real live game, or following a specially laid scent line or 'drag'.

Today 'man's best friend', the dog, has had every one of its instincts and natural abilities exploited. It is used in all manner of work from sledding to guiding the blind and in sports ranging from racing to retrieving game. Perhaps the most important of all canine roles, though, is that of the pet and companion, in which the dog provides an enigmatic mysterious comforter, a silent confidante, mentor and friend.

Hounds and Gundogs

HOUNDS

Long before the invention of firearms, man enlisted the aid of his dogs in hunting down all sorts of game. At first this was in order to provide food for himself and his family, but later, as the hunter developed into the agriculturalist, man also learned to hunt for sport. Today there are two quite distinct groups of hounds, the long-legged, racy hounds that hunt by sighting their prey before catching and killing it, and those which follow a subtle scent. This second category includes most of the pack hunting dogs, as well as the short-legged types which are able to follow their quarry underground.

Sight Hounds One sight hound, which has retained the type of its remote ancestors to the present day, is the majestic GREYHOUND. This fact is readily verified by examining Ancient Egyptian wall decorations made over 5000 years ago. Although it is probably best known today for its role as a canine racing machine, regularly entertaining many thousands of dog-track enthusiasts throughout the world, the Greyhound has a wonderful temperament and kind nature. This makes the breed very easy to lead and house-train, and perfect as a show dog. For prize-winning potential, the Greyhound must be strongly built and generously proportioned, averaging 65 lb (29 kg) in weight with a long head and neck, deep chest, arched loins and powerful hindquarters. The skull is flat with a fair width between the neat, backward-swept ears. The dark eyes look bright and intelligent.

Like a scaled-down Greyhound, the WHIPPET, about 20 inches (50 cm) high,

A pack of working BEAGLES is generally hunted on foot, its quarry being the hare.

11

Above: The GREYHOUND
has remained virtually
unchanged through history,
large, strong and extremely
fast.

Right: WHIPPETS were once
known as the working
man's greyhound, but
became a noted breed in
their own right.

12

is also capable of great speed. The Whippet was first developed in the industrial areas of England to catch rabbits for the cooking pot and for racing at weekends. It proved easier and more economical to keep, taking up less room indoors than the Greyhound, and to this day has remained a healthy, hardy and affectionate pet. The show Whippet must be strongly built, combining muscular power with elegance of outline and should move with great freedom of action. The long fine head is flat on top with a tapered muzzle, and is quite wide between the bright, alert eyes. The tiny ears are rose-shaped and never pricked. The long arched neck is set into oblique shoulders, and the back arches and the quarters show that this dog is built for speed.

Dogs of Greyhound type were developed in several countries east of the Mediterranean and, although they varied slightly from area to area, they became known collectively as Eastern Greyhounds. In northern Afghanistan a very tall and fast long-coated dog emerged, able to withstand the extreme cold of its hilly homeland and able to hunt efficiently. The AFGHAN HOUND was trained to find and run down antelope, often working in conjunction with a trained hawk which could sight the quarry from its airborne vantage point, then swoop down to indicate the exact location to its canine partner. Today the Afghan is perhaps the most glamorous of all show dogs, its long silky coat flowing as it trots gracefully in the ring. Possessing a general appearance of strength, speed and dignity, the Afghan dog should stand 27 inches (68·5 cm) high – the bitch should be 2 inches (50 mm) shorter. The profuse coat may be any colour. It should flow over the shoulders, flanks and quarters but be

The AFGHAN HOUND has a long profuse coat which needs very regular grooming.

13

short on the foreface and the back. The almost triangular eyes should be dark and the low-set ears are covered with very long, silky hair.

The SALUKI, or Gazelle-hound, was originally trained, like the Afghan, to hunt with the help of a hawk. Like all the Greyhounds it is built for speed and stamina. The Saluki was bred for generations by nomadic Bedouin tribesmen who considered the animal more sacred than their valuable hawks and fine horses. Recognized by the American Kennel Club in 1927, the Saluki has proved a popular and consistent show dog. It should be 23 to 28 inches (58–71 cm) in height and can be white, cream, fawn, golden, red, grizzle, tan, black and tan or tri-coloured.

In the Highlands of Scotland, the terrain necessitated the development of a different sort of Greyhound for keeping

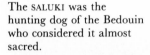

The SALUKI was the hunting dog of the Bedouin who considered it almost sacred.

the large herds of red deer in check. Eventually a very tall breed emerged, efficient at its work, obedient and biddable to its master. With its harsh and wiry weatherproof coat, the SCOTTISH DEERHOUND is a perfect product of its environment, but it is fairly rare in the show ring. It is bred in several colours, with a dark blue-grey being preferred; any white markings are heavily penalized.

In Ireland a similar dog was bred to hunt the Irish elk, a particularly large species of deer, often standing as high as a horse. Because the big fearless dog would also tackle wolves, it became known as the IRISH WOLFHOUND. Tallest of all today's pedigree dogs, the Wolfhound has a commanding appearance, less massive than the Great Dane, but heavier than the Scottish Deerhound. It has a rough coat, especially wiry over the eyes and under the jaw, and may be grey, brindle, black, pure white or fawn.

The Wolfhound of Russian origin is called the BORZOI and was first brought out of the country of its birth in the late 19th century. A popular show dog, the Borzoi is tall and stately, with a beautiful waved or curled coat which responds well to expert grooming.

All the tall sight hounds require special care if they are to be kept as pets. They must have methodical training from an early age and have the facilities to take sufficient running exercise to keep fit and healthy as adults. They need a lot of good quality food and are, therefore, expensive to keep. However, they make very impressive companions and their sheer size is generally enough to deter would-be intruders.

Scent Hounds Through the centuries hounds which hunt by scent were selectively bred to hunt specific types of prey. The ENGLISH FOXHOUND has a well-documented history, dating back to the 13th century. Dogs in the earliest packs varied greatly in size and conformation but careful breeding techniques and exchanges of stock between the country estates gradually produced an efficient type of hound of fairly uniform size and colouring.

In 1650 pairs of English Foxhounds were brought across the Atlantic and eventually the AMERICAN FOXHOUND

Francehill Pola Bear of Edgeelmclere is a red-and-white BORZOI or RUSSIAN WOLFHOUND, proud and majestic.

developed. The breed was strengthened by further importations from England and France late in the 18th century, and again improved with some Irish stock, including the Kerry Beagle, being introduced some years later. As the American Foxhound is used for four different purposes, four slightly different types of hound are bred. For pack hunting the Foxhound needs a combination of speed, stamina and the ability to jump or climb obstacles, a good bell-like voice, an excellent nose and the temperament to live and work within a pack. For field trials speed becomes the most important characteristic because such events are timed. For hunting the fox with a gun the hound's voice is all important, for the huntsman must be able to locate the quarry for a clear shot. Trial or drag hounds need extra speed and stamina. Foxhounds are independent and wilful by nature, and although very friendly and affectionate, their pack instincts make them unsuitable for life as normal family pets. It is possible, however, for

knowledgeable people living near hunt kennels, to take a puppy for rearing until it is old enough to be entered into the pack. Puppy walkers, as such people are called, raise the young dogs in their own family, and often take in new recruits when their 'old' puppies return to kennels.

The BLACK AND TAN COONHOUND is thought to have descended from the Kerry Beagle, imported from Ireland early in the 19th century. The Irish dog was typically black-and-tan in colour, a tough, agile sporting dog, now extinct. The Coonhound can trail most types of game, but has been specifically trained over many years, to hunt raccoon and opossum, two species of nocturnal climbing animals. The Coonhound seeks out and follows the scent, hunting as efficiently by night as by day, and eventually trees its quarry, loudly baying until the huntsman arrives on the scene.

Although it remains a hunting dog, the Black and Tan Coonhound was accepted by the American Kennel Club

15

Above: FOXHOUNDS hunt in well-ordered packs to track down their quarry the fox, following centuries-old tradition.

Right: The BEAGLE has become a popular pet and show dog, well-behaved and affectionate.

in 1945 and its official show standard was devised. About 25 inches (63·5 cm) in height, the dogs are powerfully built and fairly long in the legs with the typical hound head and very long, low-set ears. The coat is short, dense and hard-wearing, coal black over most of the body, but with rich tan markings above the eyes, on the muzzle, chest and legs.

Looking rather like a scaled-down version of the Foxhound, the HARRIER is, in fact, a quite separate breed and has been used in the United States for hunting the hare since colonial times. Today, the breed is accepted for show purposes by the American Kennel Club and judges look for a compact, muscular dog about 20 inches (51 cm) high, full of quality with typical hound conformation and colouring.

Even smaller than the Harrier and of similar appearance is the BEAGLE. For showing purposes the Beagle is accepted in two sizes: there are classes for dogs under 13 inches (33 cm) high and for those over 13 inches. Although a typical pack hound, and very efficient when kept expressly for hunting the hare, the Beagle has also proved to be a good house pet and was the most popular show dog in the United States for a while. Being a true hound, however, the Beagle, though clean, intelligent and affectionate, can be extremely wilful and may totally disregard its owner's voice when distracted or engaged in its own business.

16

Left: The BASSET HOUND is heavier, a large dog on shortish legs, with a big bell-like bark and a protective nature.

A litter of rare OTTERHOUND puppies.

Another breed which has gained unprecedented favour in the show ring and as a pet is the BASSET HOUND. Bred for trailing deer, hares and rabbits, it originated in France where several different versions exist today. The Basset is a big hound on short legs, so that it stands only about 14 inches (35·5 cm) tall. Usually wilful with a very independent nature, a pet Basset must have lots of exercise to prevent obesity, and needs correct early training to ensure at least a modicum of obedience. It is a very affectionate quiet dog and loves children, but may be wary of strangers.

Biggest and strongest of the scent hounds is the majestic BLOODHOUND which is thought to have descended from the black St Hubert's Hounds, brought from the Holy Land to France centuries ago. The Bloodhound has the supreme scenting ability and can follow trails laid several days before, and over very long distances. In the 17th century such hounds were used in England to track down sheep stealers and other criminals, and they were later used extensively by police forces in other countries. In the United States the Bloodhound was valued for tracking runaway slaves but, despite its powerful frame and formidable size, stories of Bloodhounds injuring fugitives are untrue as the breed is renowned for its docility and gentleness.

Probably descended from the Bloodhound, the great, shaggy-coated OTTERHOUND is just as friendly and affectionate and was originally bred to hunt otters, a tough aquatic mammal which once threatened game fish in English rivers.

Rare in its homeland, the Otterhound is accepted for showing in the United States, and is valued as a companion, guard and watchdog.

Two African breeds of hound have been accepted as show dogs and pets. The RHODESIAN RIDGEBACK, descended from dogs of Southern Africa, has been described by a 16th-century writer on an essay on domestic animals as 'an ugly creature being shaped like that of a jackal and the hair in his spine being turned foward; but he was a faithful serviceable animal of his kind.' The unusual hair formation has been passed down through the generations, and even today the Ridgeback has its characteristic ridge which by giving the impression of having its hackles perpetually raised adds to its rather fierce appearance. These dogs were first called Lion Dogs and were used to help hunt the King of Beasts, tracking and holding the

animal at bay until the arrival of the hunters. The modern Rhodesian Ridgeback is used both as a guard and as a hunting dog in its homeland, but in the Western world, it has made its name as an excellent watchdog, show dog and family pet. Allowed only a distinctive range of golden colouring, known officially as light wheaten to red wheaten, this dog, standing 26 inches (66 cm) at the shoulder and powerfully built, looks impressive and is totally fearless.

The other African hound is the prick-eared and ring-tailed BASENJI, a smart neat dog which is only about 17 inches (43 cm) high but full of courage and personality. The Basenji is unique as it is unable to bark; it makes only a soft yodelling call when it wishes to show pleasure or in greeting. This breed was developed by the natives of the Congo, and hunted in packs, driving game into catch nets. Such hunting dogs were

The impressive RHODESIAN RIDGEBACK has an unusual raised ridge of hair along its withers, adding to its impressive appearance.

18

Left: This ELKHOUND puppy is prepared to protect his territory, even at this tender age.

Below: *Kingsway Bit of Class* is a red-and-white BASENJI, a barkless African breed.

highly prized by their owners, and were well cared for but eventually a few were sold for export. Shown for the first time in England in 1937 as Congo Terriers, the early Basenji stock succumbed to infectious disease, but gradually the breed increased in numbers and improved in stamina. The Basenji Club of America was founded in 1942 and the Bansenji has become a popular show dog. Its endearing habit of washing itself like a cat, has ensured it a welcome place in the home. The Basenji has a short fine and very sleek coat which may be either bright red, pure black or black and tan. The feet, chest and tip of tail are white and it may also have white legs, blaze and collar markings. The tail is set high and curls tightly over the spine in typical Spitz fashion.

19

Far right: DACHSHUNDS of all sizes and coat types make perfect family pets, intelligent, playful and quite fearless.

Right: The FINNISH SPITZ looks rather like a furry red fox. It is a delightful breed, making an obedient, odour-free housepet.

There are two other hounds which belong in the Spitz group. The largest, weighing about 50 lb (23 kg), is the NORWEGIAN ELKHOUND, an old Scandinavian type bred for hunting and baying the great elk. A friendly alert dog, the Elkhound has retained the big bell-like voice of its ancestors. The animal is easy to train and makes a superb show dog although the thick, coarse, abundant coat is apt to shed constantly if the dog is kept too warm.

Just as the Elkhound is always grey, so the slightly smaller FINNISH SPITZ is always red. Raised originally to hunt and mark birds in trees, this Spitz is not recognized by the American Kennel Club, but makes a perfect house dog and is especially good with children. It is generally well-behaved and has no doggy odour.

The smallest hounds are the DACHSHUNDS which have spread from their native Germany to become popular show dogs and pets all over the world. First known as the Teckel, a smooth-coated dog with longer legs than the modern Dachshund, the breed is now found in both standard and miniature sizes, and in three coat types: the Long-Haired, the Smooth-Haired and the Wire-Haired. The original Teckel was used for hunting fox and hare in packs, and also for seeking animals which had gone to ground. Selection was gradually made for shorter legs and the longer body as seen today. Independent, intelligent, loving and loyal, it is not surprising that this breed has proved perhaps the most popular of all the hounds in making the difficult transition from hunter to pet.

20

Right: An ENGLISH POINTER fixes the position of game while working in the field.

Below: The GERMAN WIREHAIRED POINTER makes a good housedog as well as an efficient worker.

GUNDOGS

Dogs now known as gundogs started their diversification long before the gun was invented, but so successful were they in seeking out and dealing with certain types of game, that they have remained in their allotted and well-earned niches to this day.

Two groups locate game for hunters and sportsmen. These are the pointers and the setters. Pointers work by coming to the point, standing rigidly, often with one foot raised in mid-stride. When two dogs are used as coordinates, the exact location of the squatting bird or hare is easily found. When setters locate game, they 'set', sinking to the ground, noses towards their quarry. Spaniels move game, either putting birds up into the air for the guns, or running them along the ground. Different breeds are used for working different types of country or terrain.

Retrievers are mostly large strong dogs capable of working through the roughest undergrowth to retrieve fallen game. A few breeds have evolved as all-purpose gundogs. Each sportsman will argue that his breed is the finest in the world, but it is true to say that every breed has its own virtues in the field.

Pointers The modern POINTER is one of the most handsome of all sporting dogs, with its short smooth coat, often striking markings and powerful, muscular lines. The GERMAN SHORT-HAIRED

POINTER is of similar build, but has a longer muzzle and half-docked tail. It makes a fine dual-purpose pointer-retriever and an excellent watchdog, unlike many of the gundogs which appear to love everyone, including complete strangers. The GERMAN WIRE-HAIRED POINTER was developed in order to produce an all-round utility gundog and resulted in a tough, enthusiastic and hard-working animal, similar in shape to the Short-haired Pointer but with a dense wiry coat.

Setters Setters, with their beautiful coats and long silky feathering on the ears, legs and tail, make loving pets and glamorous show stars as well as being highly efficient sporting dogs. The IRISH SETTER was bred from small setting spaniels during the 18th century, and is the smallest setter breed. A gay spirited dog, it is a rich glowing chestnut in colour, with dark brown or hazel, almond-shaped eyes. The ENGLISH SETTER is very similar in build to its Irish cousin and was first bred from the same root-stock in 1825. It is basically white with coloured flecks or markings of either blue, lemon, orange or liver.

Heaviest of the group is the rarely seen GORDON SETTER, first bred to work in the craggy Highlands of Scotland at the end of the 18th century. The breed's founder was the fourth Duke of Gordon, who made the initial cross between a setter and a black-and-tan collie. Today's Gordon Setter is a strong, muscular dog, coal black in colour with chestnut markings over the eyes and on the muzzle, throat, chest and legs.

ENGLISH SETTERS make model mothers. This calm bitch keeps company with her pretty blue Belton pup.

23

LABRADOR RETRIEVERS are easily trained to reach demanding standards as gundogs and in trials.

Retrievers Retrievers are all built on similar lines and are large, active dogs with strong backs and necks, and mouths so gentle that they do not mark the game they carry back to their masters. The LABRADOR RETRIEVER is kind and gentle, smooth-coated and perhaps the most popular of all gundogs as a pet and house dog. It is a fairly recent breed, first used in Newfoundland to help fishermen pulling in their nets. Today it makes an ideal sporting dog and its high intelligence and trainability have made it ideal for police work and as a guide dog for the blind.

From a pair of Newfoundland dogs shipwrecked off the coast of Maryland in 1807, a new breed came into being. Called the CHESAPEAKE BAY RETRIEVER, its special waved and naturally oily coat is water-repellant, making this dog ideal for retrieving game birds from cold waters. A steady and reliable worker, the Chesapeake Bay Retriever is very protective of its home and family and does not like strangers. It is rarely seen at shows, possibly because it looks a real worker and is rather unglamorous. The Chesapeake's unusual and distinctive coat ranges in colour from that of dead grass to dark tan and is ideal for a water dog, blending as it does with the reeds.

From the Labrador and Newfoundland, with later additions of Gordon and

24

Irish Setter blood, came the FLAT-COATED RETRIEVER, selectively bred for retrieving from water. It has had fluctuating popularity over the years, but is now well-established as a show dog and makes a wonderful house dog as long as it gets sufficient exercise. Usually coal black, but occasionally seen in deep liver colour, the coat is dense, but fine in texture and close-lying with a little feathering on the ears, legs and tail.

Also black or liver in colour is the rare CURLY-COATED RETRIEVER, a breed which has remained virtually unchanged since its production from the ancient breed of Water Dog, many years ago. Its thick, curly coat enables this dog to work in very dense undergrowth and insulates the animal against both wet and cold.

In 1868 a breeding programme was commenced by Lord Tweedmouth which resulted in the production of a fine dog which has become extremely popular throughout the world and is

A CHESAPEAKE BAY RETRIEVER pup looking slightly bemused by its training lure.

This GOLDEN RETRIEVER puppy anxiously waits for a word of praise during its early training.

25

known as the GOLDEN RETRIEVER. This dog excels in field work, is quiet and gentle as a family pet, and its high intelligence has made it ideal as a guide dog and in obedience tests. The feathered coat repays proper care and grooming, and may be of any shade of gold or cream.

Spaniels Spaniels hunt close to their handlers, exploring the ground cover in order to flush out any game which may be hidden there. When the bird or animal bursts out and is shot, the dog must then wait, retrieving it only on command.

The Spaniel family dates back to the fourteenth century when it was divided into Land Spaniels and Water Spaniels. The IRISH WATER SPANIEL has a coat of tight ringlets and walks well in marshy land.

The ENGLISH SPRINGER SPANIEL is used for working and as a show dog, and is perhaps the most popular of all dual-purpose gundogs, well-behaved in the house and a tireless worker on land and in the water.

Two types of Cocker Spaniel are found in the United States are are bred along quite different lines. The ENGLISH COCKER is a popular pet and working dog and has been bred for almost 100

Above: The ENGLISH SPRINGER SPANIEL is always willing and hoping to please, whether working or just being the friend of the family.

Right: Two winsome COCKER SPANIEL puppies from the Bidston Kennels await collection by their new owners.

26

Invernieti Gaiety Girl is an attractive tricolour COCKER SPANIEL bitch.

years. It gained its name in 1801 when Land Spaniels were first divided into two groups: the Starters were used for springing game to be taken by falcons and other trained hawks; and the Cockers were specially trained for hunting woodcock, a small game bird.

The AMERICAN COCKER is shown with a more abundant coat that its English cousin, and this is specially prepared to stand out around the legs and at the base of ears. It moves gaily and well and like most spaniels has a loving and pleasing personality.

The CLUMBER SPANIEL is very distinctive, with a massive head and a dignified, thoughtful expression. It is an ancient breed which has not changed over the years, but has become rare although it is a good worker and a friendly and affectionate pet. The Clumber has an abundant coat with silky feathering and is generally white with lemon markings, a speckled muzzle and soulful eyes of deep amber.

Another rare member of this group is the SUSSEX SPANIEL, a slow but conscientious worker with the unusual habit of giving tongue in his deep melodious voice when on the trail. Short in the leg and sturdily built, the Sussex Spaniel has a flat, abundant coat of rich golden liver, shading to pure gold at the tips.

The FIELD SPANIEL is a self-coloured dog with tan markings, longer in the leg, larger and generally more active than the Cocker. It makes a good all-round worker and family pet and, like most spaniels, is intelligent, obedient and easily trained.

27

This magnificent
HUNGARIAN VIZSLA gets
ready for the judges at
London's famous Cruft's
Dog Show.

Other Gundogs Two unusual sporting dogs are the WEIMARANER and the HUNGARIAN VIZSLA, both of which have become extremely popular in recent years as pets, workers and in the show ring.

The Weimaraner is often called the Grey Ghost because of its very distinctive silver-grey colour. First bred at the great sportsman's Court of Weimar, in Germany during the 19th century and called the Weimar Pointer, this large, speedy, brave dog was used for tracking, scenting, retrieving and bringing large animals to bay. Jealously guarded by German breeders, it was not until 1929 that the first Weimaraners were brought to the United States where it quickly gained popularity.

The Vizsla is a tall but lightly built, muscular dog, deep russet in colour. It was accepted by the American Kennel Club in 1960. Since that time it has become a very well-established breed, and is an aristocratic dog of noble bearing. Like the Weimaraner, the Vizsla has a short, hard coat and has its tail partially docked.

28

Working and Non-sporting Dogs

The most popular pedigree dog in the world is the ALSATIAN or GERMAN SHEP-HERD DOG, first bred from the intelligent sheepdogs of Bavaria over a hundred years ago. Highly intelligent and responsive to correct early training and kindness, dogs of this breed are in great demand for police, security and military duties and excel in obedience work. It is a large breed to keep in the house, and the heavy coat needs regular attention, but properly raised, it is a peerless pet and fearless family guard.

Another German breed which is used in security and guard work is the DOBERMANN, developed from Pinschers and Rottweilers in 1870. Further outcrosses were made with herding dogs, and eventually the fast and muscular Dobermann of today emerged. The short smooth coat is easy to keep in top condition, but the Dobermann can be very wilful and disobedient unless properly trained and handled.

The ROTTWEILER is more heavily built than its Dobermann descendants and gets it name from the town of Rottweil where it was developed as 'the butcher's dog'. Butchers used such dogs to carry large sums of money, tied securely around their necks, on cattle buying trips far from their home towns; on the return journey, the dogs worked as drovers. Today the Rottweiler makes an impressive and loyal guard and is black with rich tan markings.

Shadow, a fully trained GERMAN SHEPHERD, being 'sent away'.

Far left: Black and Tan DOBERMANNS, a mother and son, whose ears have been left naturally uncropped but still manage to look suitably impressive.

Left: A summer idyll – a boy and his BOXER enjoy a day's fishing along the riverbank.

Below: This winsome BULLMASTIFF puppy will soon grow into a massive adult, totally fearless and easily trained.

The BOXER was developed in Germany from small mastiff breeds which were used as bull-baiting dogs and, by the end of the century, had become an established and popular dog both in the home and at the earliest dog shows. The breed has remained extremely successful in the showring. The Boxer is a wonderful pet, especially good with children, who enjoy sharing its often boisterous games.

Sharing the Mastiff group with the Boxer are several more popular breeds which range in size from the Boston Terrier to the Great Dane. The MASTIFF, itself, has a long history. The name was first recorded as early as 1251, when poachers were charged in an English court with killing a doe with 'two griehounds and black mastive'. Dogs of similar type have been found on Ancient Egyptian and Assyrian wall reliefs and were obviously used for hunting and as dogs of war. Today's Mastiff is a very large and powerful but gentle giant. Although it will fiercely protect the home and property against intruders, it is faithful and loving to the family.

The BULLMASTIFF is an offshoot of the English Mastiff, smaller, and with a head showing the influence of early outcrosses to Bulldogs. Such dogs were referred to by Buffon in 1791, and in the 19th century Bullmastiff dogs were matched in the pits against all manner of animals, including lions.

Today's BULLDOGS have been selectively bred to accentuate certain features, and are quite unlike their bullbaiting ancestors of yesteryear.

The BULLDOG is the national dog of Britain. An ancient breed, it was first developed for the sport of bull-baiting (which finally became illegal in 1835). Selective breeding has gradually accentuated the dog's features, until it is now, basically, a show dog for the connoisseur.

The FRENCH BULLDOG has been known in its native land since the 17th century. It is said to have originated from the great Dogue de Bordeaux which was miniaturized to produce both Bulldogs and French Bulldogs. The breed was adopted in the United States over a hundred years ago and soon gained popularity. It is a dog with a delightful temperament, so charming, quaint and intelligent that it soon becomes an inte-

gral part of the family into which it has been accepted as a pet.

The BOSTON TERRIER is not a terrier at all, and is recognized by most countries as being the national dog of America, even though his ancestors came originally from Britain. The first Boston was a dog called Hooper's Judge, produced from a Bulldog and an English Terrier. From this dark brindle dog with its white throat and blaze, cropped ears and screw-tail, careful breeding eventually produced the compact and stylish Boston Terrier of today. By 1878 the little dogs had become very popular and were shown at the Boston Show, but when the American Bull Terrier Club of Boston applied for official acceptance in 1891, it was refused until the name was changed to the Boston Terrier Club, which was finally accomplished in 1893. The dapper Boston makes an ideal show dog being easy to train, prepare and transport. It is a perfect pet dog, too, loves children and plays the clown by performing many endearing tricks of its own invention.

Although the tallest of the Mastiff group is called the GREAT DANE, the breed is more likely to have been developed in Germany than in Denmark, for it was known as the *Deutsche Dogge* at one time and is still called *Dogo Alemanes* in Spain today. Very large and rather short-lived, the Great Dane is not the ideal house dog although it has a very good temperament and is kind to children and other pets. For show purposes, dogs must stand at least 32 inches (81 cm) high – bitches 30 inches (76 cm) – and the short sleek coat may be brindle, fawn, blue, black or harlequin, which is pure white with black, or occasionally blue, patches.

A big black mastiff-type of dog evolved in Newfoundland, Canada, which had probably descended from the

Above: The FRENCH BULLDOG, *Donna Dale Miss Rose Bud,* shows off the good features of her breed.

Left: Champion BOSTON TERRIER *Balleris Johnny Go Lightly* displays his show stance.

33

Right: This magnificent
NEWFOUNDLAND is the
colour variety known as
'Landseer'.

Above: The great PYRENEAN
MOUNTAIN DOG is a natural
shepherd breed which has
readily adapted to life in
the home.

heavyweight dog, and truly at home in the water, where it has been responsible for many acts of lifesaving and rescue.

The PYRENEAN MOUNTAIN DOG has also descended from the Tibetan Mastiff and its predominantly white, profuse coat effectively protected it against extremes of weather in the high mountains of its original home, where it fiercely guarded flocks against attack by wolves and other enemies.

Another big mastiff is the ST BERNARD, famous for its work in finding travellers lost in the high mountain passes of the Alps. This breed of dog is one of the heaviest in the world and takes up a lot of room in the home as well as consuming large amounts of food. Like most of the very large dogs, the St Bernard must have sympathetic treatment and correct training, and it will make a good companion, fearsome guard, and dignified show dog.

Also from Switzerland is the BERNESE MOUNTAIN DOG, an old breed once used for draught purposes by the basket weavers and cheese makers of Berne. A lovable and kindly dog, easily trained and obedient, the Bernese Mountain Dog soon found a place in the United States and was accepted by the American Kennel Club in 1930.

Modern-day draught-dog breeds include the ALASKAN MALAMUTE and the SIBERIAN HUSKY, both renowned for their endurance, strength and ability to pull

Tibetan Mastiff although its origins are obscure. By 1860 some of these NEWFOUNDLAND dogs had been taken to Britain and six were entered in the Birmingham Show where they caused great interest. A few of the Newfoundlands were white with black markings, and one such dog was painted by the most famous of all animal artists, Sir Edwin Landseer, from whom they took their varietal name. Today's Newfoundland is accepted in black, chocolate or bronze and Landseer. It is a very big,

34

Left: The BERNESE MOUNTAIN DOG, originally a herder and draught dog, needs lots of exercise.

Below: Harnessed HUSKIES eagerly await the signal to move off over the frozen snow.

35

Above: The SAMOYED is of Spitz type, with a very profuse snow-white coat.

heavily laden sleds over difficult terrain in sub-zero temperatures.

The SAMOYED is another Spitz breed originally used for draught work as well as hunting bear in its native land, although the pure-white show Samoyed of today is a very refined version of its ancestors.

The golden-coloured CHOW CHOW is a Spitz with a difference, for it is the descendant of Chinese dogs once raised for the table, and considered a great delicacy. It is an aloof, one-person type of dog and can be difficult to train in the accepted sense, although it makes a spectacular show dog.

The DALMATIAN was originally a hunting and guard dog in Dalmatia or Croatia, and probably developed from the harlequin-coloured Great Danes crossed with pointers to reduce size and improve markings. The breed's beautifully spotted white coat and elegant lines soon ensured a great gain in popularity, especially as a lady's companion and personal guard. By the Victorian era in

Right: The DALMATIAN should have distinct spots and is a very handsome dog. Once used to guard carriages, it used to run between the wheels.

36

England, the Dalmatian had become a carriage dog, living in the stables and accompanying the carriage, trotting either at the side of the horses or under the rear axle. For many years the Dalmatian has been associated with the Fire Service in the United States. In fact, the Dalmatian appears on the American Fire Department's badge. The Dalmatian has also proved popular in stage and circus acts throughout the world. In a show dog the distinctive spots may be either black or liver-coloured and must not form large patches. The nose must match the spots, and dogs must not exceed 24 inches (61 cm) in height.

The POODLE has also had a long association with stage and circus performers and is a natural clown with a wonderful sense of fun. In most countries Poodles are divided into three varieties by size. American Kennel Club requirements call for the Standard Poodle to be over 15 inches (38 cm) in height, the Miniature to be 10–15 inches (26–38 cm) tall and the Toy under 10 inches (26 cm). Apart from their height, all the Poodles have similar characteristics, and are elegant, active and intelligent. The profuse coat is kept clipped, even in pet dogs, and for showing, special traditional clipping patterns must be used. The Standard Poodle was originally a gundog, descended from the Water Dog or Pudel of Germany. In the old days the coat was probably oiled and persuaded to form long cords. Gradually, selective breeding for small size produced the Miniature, and eventually the Toy. Poodles like to be part of the family and hate being confined to kennels. They are good guards, barking fiercely at strangers, and adore members of their own human family.

Two Hungarian breeds of herding dogs have long corded coats: the small generally dark-coated PULI and the large white KOMONDOR. The Puli, like the Poodle, has descended from the Water Dog and is very hardy, active, easily trained and possessed of herding abilities. It was first imported into the United

Beneath his fancy trim, the STANDARD POODLE is a real he-man of a dog, highly intelligent, very faithful and a wonderful guard.

37

Right: The HUNGARIAN PULI pup *Ockley Sage* smiles to show a super set of teeth.

Below: Like the small dark PULI, the large white KOMONDOR has an unusual corded coat.

States in the early 1930s, and gained official recognition as part of the Working Group in 1936. The Komondor reached the United States at about the same time and was recognized in 1937 but has remained rare, possibly due to the demands made to prepare the corded coat for the show ring. Like many of the older working breeds, the Komondor is highly intelligent and responds to correct training, making a fine herder and guard dog.

Renowned in France as a herder and guardian of the flocks is the BRIARD which takes its name from the Province of Brie. During the First World War, American troops saw and admired dogs of the breed and this resulted in its introduction to the United States at the end of hostilities. The Briard has a long, slightly waved coat, which may be of any solid colour or with the effect called *charbonnée* in which the longer guard hairs are each tipped with black. The coat is easy to prepare for showing, and although of strong character, the Briard is responsive to training, well mannered and makes a very good guard dog.

The BOUVIER DES FLANDRES looks the true working dog that it is, compact, powerful and with a rugged unkempt coat of any colour from fawn to black, salt and pepper, grey and brindle. The name Bouvier translates to mean 'cowherd' or 'oxherd', and the breed was first used to drive cattle purchased by butchers. Today's Bouvier makes a superb guard, and a large, smart show dog.

Belgium has produced three fine breeds of sheep herding dogs all rather similar to the German Shepherd dog in their general conformation. The GROENENDAHL is jet black, its powerful body covered with long, coarse hair dense over the body and extra long and abundant around the neck, down the backs of the legs and fringing the tail. It was originally bred in the village of Groenendahl. The first black puppies were brought to the United States in 1907 and the breed has steadily gained ground as the perfect house dog and a scene-stealer at shows.

The MALINOIS first reached American shores in 1948, but until 1959 it was shown simply as one of a group of Belgian Shepherd dogs. Eventually, however, the distinctive dog was recognized

38

Left: The BOUVIER DES FLANDRES is a strong fearless dog, originally used for working cattle but now an effective guard.

Below: The tall ear placement of the impressive GROENENDAHL adds to his alert expression.

in its own right as the Belgian Malinois. It has a shorter coat than the Groenendahl, and is dark fawn in colour with a considerable amount of black overlaying the powerfully built body and with a dark mask and ears. It is a rather reserved dog and does not readily accept strangers, making it an efficient guard.

The third in this group of sheepdogs is the BELGIAN TERVUEREN, another large, prick-eared breed with an abundant coat, a warm mahogany in colour overlaid with black. The breed has made slow progress since its independent registration by the American Kennel Club in 1959, but it has retained superb herding ability, and is highly responsive to training for obedience, for work, and for the show ring.

The COLLIE was one of the first pure-bred herd dogs to be imported into the United States of America from Britain and both the Rough and Smooth-coated varieties were represented at the earliest of the Amercian dog shows. The present standard calls for dogs to be about 25 inches (63·5 cm) in height. Four colours are recognized: sable-and-white, tri-colour, blue-merle and white. Collies excel as show dogs and make intelligent and easily trained protective pets. They need

39

Pebhallows Puddle Jumper is a beautiful slate-and-white BEARDED COLLIE, his coat groomed for the show.

lots of running exercise to keep trim, and the coat of the Rough variety requires regular grooming, especially for the show ring.

OLD ENGLISH SHEEPDOGS have been bred for years, but gradually the working potential and characteristics of the breed have been sacrificed in the quest for glamorous show traits. Today's standard requires the dog to be about 22 inches (56 cm) tall and totally tailless with a profuse hard-textured coat and hair covering the face.

The SHETLAND SHEEPDOG is a miniature collie-type dog, first bred in the Shetland Islands off the north coast of Scotland, where the harsh inhospitable climate has produced reduced versions of several species including dogs, ponies and sheep. Though small in stature, the Shetland Sheepdog is essentially a working breed and should never look frail or weedy. It is very popular as a show dog, and its profuse coat repays proper grooming. A happy, alert and friendly breed, the 'Sheltie' makes a fine family

40

Left: The OLD ENGLISH SHEEPDOG has become extremely popular as a pet, but few owners realize the care required for the very profuse coat.

Below: Another cattledog that gained favour in the home is the WELSH CORGI.

pet, and trains well for obedience work and competitions.

Two varieties of WELSH CORGI exist: the popular short-tailed Pembroke, and the comparatively rare long-tailed Cardigan. Apart from their tails, the two breeds are very similar in appearance, and it remains a mystery as to why one has found favour and the other has not. The Queen of England keeps several Pembroke Corgies which may account in part for their popularity. The Pembroke is slightly smaller than the Cardigan and may be red, sable, fawn, or black-and-tan and may or may not have white markings on the legs, chest and neck. Cardigan Corgies may be any colour except white and have very large erect ears. The Corgi was used centuries ago for driving herds of cattle on long journeys to market and protecting them from footpads and thieves. Today the Corgi is still used on the small hill farms of Wales, the land of its birth, but has also found favour as a family pet and companion. It makes a fine show dog.

Terriers, Toys and Tiny Tibetans

BULL TERRIER puppies whose innocent looks belie their true intent are *Quillon Mowgli, Quincey* and *Caliph*.

Terriers get their definitive name from *terra*, the Latin word for earth, which refers to their innate inclination to dig and go to ground after their quarry. Early terriers were roughly divided into two types, and a writer of 1677 described those of his day in depth. He mentioned terriers with short coats and crooked legs, ideal for going underground and fearless in the face of a fox or badger, and those with longer legs and shaggy coats, which would not only fiercely enter the earth, but were also capable of hunting above ground. Selective breeding, often within confined regions, eventually produced a whole range of distinctive terrier breeds, each well-equipped to work over its own type of terrain after specific game or vermin.

Toy dogs, unlike most of the other non-sporting breeds, have been bred mainly as perfect tiny pets. They were often called sleeve dogs, pillow dogs or comforters, and were kept by well-to-do lonely women as companions while their husbands were away hunting or fighting.

Right: BULL TERRIERS can be wilful as puppies but mature into magnificent guards.

Below: Here a family of AMERICAN BULL TERRIER adults and puppies romp in the yard.

Sleeve dogs nestled inside a lady's wide sleeves, a notion copied from the Pekingese sleeve dogs which fitted inside a mandarin's robes. The pillow dog slept at the head of the bed at night, and the extra warmth of its little body attracted fleas and lice from its mistress to itself. The comforters were employed to warm their owners' hands and feet, or placed on the lap to help ease abdominal pains. Fashionable folk soon vied to own the most exquisite of tiny dogs, and today's many toy varieties gradually evolved.

Though it is not in itself an ancient breed, the BULL TERRIER descended from the earliest of British Terriers, notably the Old English White, which, crossed with the Bulldog in the 19th century, produced the Staffordshire Bull Terrier. From this, another early strain of pure white dogs arose and dominated the show scene in the 1860s. Sometimes described as the gladiator of the canine race, the Bull Terrier of today is strongly built and very muscular, with a keen intelligent expression. It is a fearless dog and, therefore, an excellent guard, but it can be affectionate and very good with children. The American Kennel Club does not impose height or weight limits, but white dogs must be pure white, though head markings are allowed, and coloured dogs predominately coloured – brindle is preferred.

The AMERICAN STAFFORDSHIRE TERRIER is an example of diversification of varieties for originally this Terrier and the STAFFORDSHIRE BULL TERRIER were one breed. The Staffordshire Bull Terrier was recognized in Britain by 1935, but was not accepted in the United States. The Staffordshire Terrier was, however, and its name was eventually changed to the American Staffordshire in 1972. In the meantime the Staffordshire Bull Terrier had become popular in Britain, and in 1974 it was recognized as a separate variety by the American Kennel Club. Today two breeds, quite similar in appearance and with a common ancestry, now exist side by side.

Bull Terriers were originally bred as fighting dogs, and traits such as fearlessness and aggression were selectively bred into the animals. Even today the American Staffordshire, like his British counterpart, is a very strong dog for its size, with powerful shoulders and quarters and formidable jaws. Show dogs of this breed should be about 18 inches (45 cm) high, and the short close coat may be of any solid colour, parti-colour

or patched. The British-bred Staffordshire is slightly smaller and may be red, fawn, black, blue or brindle, either self-coloured or patched with white. Pure white dogs are also allowed, but liver or black-and-tan are disqualified from the show ring. A Miniature Bull Terrier has been perfected in Britain, but has not been granted Championship status by the American Kennel Club. It is similar to the standard Bull Terrier in conformation and colouring, and has been merely scaled down in perfect proportions so that its height does not exceed 14 inches (36 cm).

The American Kennel Club recognizes the FOX TERRIER as one breed with two varieties, the Smooth and the Wire-Haired. It is said to have descended from two early English dogs, the half-coated Black-and-Tan Wire-Haired Terrier, and the smooth-coated English White Terrier. The Fox Terrier is an alert and inquisitive dog, about 15 inches (38 cm) high, predominately white with patches of colour on the body

One of the smartest of all pets is the WIRE-HAIRED FOX TERRIER, seen here in show trim and standing well.

The brightly coloured IRISH TERRIERS are full of energy and need space to play.

The SOFT-COATED WHEATEN is a gentle dog of medium size and its pretty, profuse coat does not shed hairs.

and head. The Wire-Haired variety needs regular trimming, and both types make excellent show dogs and guards.

Taller, with a hard wiry coat of a glorious red or red-wheaten colour, is the protective IRISH TERRIER. Once used to carry despatches across minefields in wartime, this loyal and brave dog is often known as the Dare-Devil, but is loving, affectionate and devoted to its master and makes a good house pet if given sufficient opportunity to exercise freely.

Another unusual Irish breed of terrier is the stylish KERRY BLUE. First discovered in the beautiful area known as the Ring of Kerry, it eventually found its way across the Atlantic and a breed club was founded in the United States of America in 1926. Since that time, the Kerry Blue has prospered as a show and

sporting dog. It is able to retrieve, and makes an excellent guard dog. The Kerry stands about 18 inches (46 cm) high and may be of any blue shade, with or without black points. Kerry puppies are born quite black, and their coats gradually lighten to the adult colour.

The third terrier native to Ireland was developed as a general purpose farm dog, capable of guarding the home and stock and keeping down the vermin. Known as the SOFT-COATED WHEATEN, this terrier has a soft, silky coat which is the colour of ripening wheat. Apart from this, it closely resembles the Kerry Blue Terrier, and both obviously share common ancestry. The Soft-Coated Wheaten has strong sporting instincts and is affectionate and confident, easily trained and good with children. The first dogs of the breed arrived on American

45

shores in 1946 and its breed club was formed most appropriately on St Patrick's Day in 1962. Since that time the breed has made steady progress, gradually gaining popularity.

Often called the King of Terriers, the AIRDALE is the tallest breed in this group, but the epithet does does not refer to its size but rather to the fact that the breed combines all the best terrier features. Originally bred for hunting in packs to catch otter in the river valleys of England's South Yorkshire, the breed took its name from the Aire valley when officially recognized in 1878. Previously known as the Waterside Terrier, the Airedale was more hound-like in those days, but gradually selective breeding has produced the squarely built, hard-coated dog of today. The dense wiry coat needs regular attention and special preparation for show purposes when it is shaped and trimmed to accentuate the dog's smart outline. In colour, the Airedale has a black or dark grizzle body

Above: The stately AIREDALE is often rightly called the 'King of Terriers'.

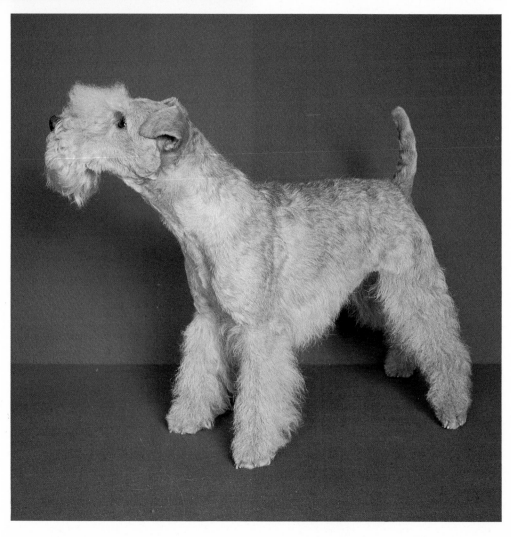

Right: This red LAKELAND TERRIER is *Louieville Red Baron*, a top winning dog.

46

with tan markings on the head and legs. A fearless dog, the Airedale has successfully been used for police work and as a war dog, and is one of the finest of canine guards.

Often regarded as a miniature Airedale is the similarly coloured WELSH TERRIER. However, although it probably has similar roots, it has quite different proportions and detail. Standing around 15 inches (38 cm) high, this game and fearless little dog is so affectionate and obedient that it adapts well to town life and also makes the perfect show dog.

The Welsh Terrier is sometimes confused with the slightly shorter LAKELAND, but although both breeds have similar harsh and wiry coat texture, their heads are quite different. The Lakeland Terrier was first bred to hunt the fox in England's Lake District, an area in which many flocks of sheep were raised and foxes posed perennial problems. However, this dog's useful size and smart appearance combined with a happy, alert nature, soon ensured it a future as a pet and show dog. Although the Lakeland may be black-and-tan like its Welsh cousin, the American Kennel Club also accept the breed in blue-and-tan, red, wheaten, red grizzle, liver, blue or black.

Another Welsh dog is the SEALYHAM which evolved late in the 19th century from various other terrier breeds. Captain John Edwardes of Sealyham in Wales wanted a short-legged strain of dogs for hunting and so picked breeding stock solely on their rat-catching abilities. From a medley of small terriers the Sealyham emerged as a distinctive breed and swiftly spread from its native land, making its Amercian show debut in California in 1911. The modern Sealyham is only about 10 inches (25 cm) high and is generally white although it may have a lemon, brown or badger-pied markings on the head. The long hard wiry coat is carefully shaped for the show ring, where this dog moves with great presence, as if conscious of its admiring audience. Possessing a large bark for its small size, the Sealyham makes an excellent house dog and is always ready and willing to entertain with games and tricks, often of its own invention.

Scotland has given birth to several terrier breeds and although it is likely

that they all stemmed from the same root stock, the country's isolated rural areas and islands ensured diversification into today's distinct types. The Scottish Terrier Club was formed in Scotland in 1882 to promote the breeding of the true SCOTTISH TERRIER, and in the United States, the American standard for the breed was agreed in 1925. A sturdy, thick-set dog with a long, noble head and short legs, the 'Scottie' has a broken, rough-textured coat which is usually black but may also be wheaten or brindle of any colour. Keen and inclined to be a little sharp, with a true terrier temperament, this is an active and very energetic breed.

Although the Scottish Terrier is said to have originated on the Island of Skye, there is, in fact, a SKYE TERRIER which differs considerably in appearance. This breed has a long straight coat and feathered tail, and may be of any self-colour with a lighter undercoat, black ears and

Micanda Flash Harry is a brindle SCOTTISH TERRIER who lives in Argentina.

47

Right: The SKYE TERRIER bitch *Fenbeach Venus* is typical of her breed, patient, loving and devoted to her owner.

Below: The CAIRN TERRIER is a game breed and always keen to go out hunting.

a black nose tip. The Skye Terrier looks glamorous, especially when the coat has been encouraged to grow and is prepared for the show ring, but this dog has great courage and its temperament is very much that of the hunter.

The CAIRN TERRIER was also developed on the Island of Skye, and was first called the Short-Haired Skye Terrier. Due to the insistence of some of the breed's founders, this little dog has retained all its true terrier characteristics despite its popularity as a show dog and pet. It was originally bred to hunt foxes in the rocky cairns of its island birthplace, and so eventually took the name, 'Cairn'. The American Kennel Club standard places great emphasis on the coat of this breed. It must be double, with profuse, hard (but not coarse) hair in the outer coat and a fur-like undercoat. The dog should weigh about 10 lb (4·5 kg) and be 10 inches (25 cm) high. It should be red, sandy, grey, brindled or almost black in colour, and may have dark ears and muzzle.

First known as the Poltalloch Terrier after the area in which its original breeder lived, the all-white terrier of Scotland was eventually accepted for official recognition as the WEST HIGHLAND WHITE TERRIER. It was first bred for hunting foxes in very rough and dif-ficult country, when a strong fearless dog was needed. Today's 'Westie' is affectionate and amusing, alert and as fearless as its ancestors, making a wonderful companion and pet as well as an ideal show dog.

Along the border country between Scotland and England a distinctive little terrier first appeared at the beginning of the 18th century. It was bred for hunting badger, fox and otter and was shown in several portraits of sporting nobleman of the time. When Sir Walter Scott's

WEST HIGHLAND WHITE TERRIERS have become very popular as housepets and are playful and very affectionate.

49

novel, *Guy Mannering*, was published in 1815, it was noted that his character, Dandie Dinmont, owned and bred very game litle sporting dogs! From that time, the breed was christened the DANDIE DINMONT TERRIER. Despite its large, dark and soulful eyes, the Dandie Dinmont is possibly the fiercest of all terriers when aroused. It can be disobedient and wilful, but is good with children and makes a superb watchdog. Long in the body and low to the ground, this dog measures from 8–11 inches (20–28 cm) at the shoulder and has an unusual coat of mixed hard and soft hair, 2 inches (50 mm) in length, which feels crisp to the hand. The breed may be either pepper or mustard in colour. The pepper ranges from dark blue-black to light silver-grey, while mustard ranges from reddish-brown to pale fawn.

Bred in the same region and from the same roots is the BORDER TERRIER. The Border Terrier, however, is much smaller and more squarely built than the Dandie Dinmont and has long legs. With the powerful jaws necessary to deal with foxes and badgers below ground, the Border Terrier is active and strong, very good with children and much quieter than others in this group. Although it is an old established breed in its homeland, this terrier has only recently

Above: The DANDIE DINMONT TERRIER is quite rare and unusual and makes a keen worker.

Right: This BORDER TERRIER *Midge* solicits a treat from her young owner.

50

arrived in the United States, where its show standard calls for a dog of about 14 lb (6 kg) in weight with a harsh, dense coat of red, wheaten, grizzle-and-tan or blue-and-tan.

With a coat and range of colours similar to the Border Terrier is the little dog first bred in England's East Anglian region and known as the NORWICH TERRIER. This neat little dog, about 10 inches (25 cm) in height, comes in two varieties, the Drop Ear and the Prick Ear. First brought to the United States just after the First World War, they were originally called Jones Terriers after their importer. The Norwich Terrier makes an active, lively pet, and having a strongly developed sense of territory, makes a good little guard dog.

The BEDLINGTON TERRIER was named by Joseph Aynsley, a mason from the north of England in 1825. Dandie Dinmont Terriers and Whippets are thought to have been used in its early develop-

ment. The breed has plenty of speed and is equally at home on land or in water. Although it was primarily bred for ratting, the Bedlington Terrier helped the family budget in olden days by catching rabbits for the cooking pot. Only over the years has its potential as a show dog been fully realized. Today the racily built Bedlington is artistically prepared for the show ring and often looks too glamorous and delicate to be a working breed. Its looks belie its nature, however, for it remains hardy and tough and is a friendly active pet. The American Kennel Club standard requires a height of about 16 inches (40·5 cm), and the very distinctive thick and linty coat should be blue, blue-and-tan, liver or sandy, and the top-knots of all adults should be lighter than the body colour.

The AUSTRALIAN TERRIER and the AUSTRALIAN SILKY TERRIER almost certainly share a common ancestry, resulting from broken-coated dogs descended from

The cuddlesome, lamb-like appearance of the BEDLINGTON belies its true terrier temperament. This superb dog is champion *Dalip Huggy Bear*.

51

Below: This alert
AUSTRALIAN TERRIER is
*Champion Mijolin's the
Hitman*, who happily
guards his home.

Bottom. YORKSHIRE
TERRIERS are large dogs in
tiny packages, bold,
courageous and very
defensive of their home.

admixtures of the Scottish and Skye
Terriers and the Dandie Dinmont. Later
the two breeds developed along separate
lines: the Silky was bred down to toy
size, while the Australian Terrier has
turned into a tough, tenacious little
hunting dog.

One of the smallest of terriers at 10
inches (25 cm) high, the Australian Terrier is used as an effective guard dog on
Australian farms and mines, and has
proved to be a popular show dog and

tidy house pet. Originally blue and tan,
Cairn Terrier blood was introduced and
a second colour was accepted, a clear
sandy red with softer top-knot.

At the Royal Melbourne Show of
1872, some very small, broken-coated
toy terriers were shown, and these were
developed by the turn of the century into
a breed called the Sydney Silky. It was
not until 1959 that the Australian
National Kennel Council accepted the
breed as the Australian Silky Terrier,
and it eventually found its way to the
United States where it is recognized as
the SILKY TERRIER. This little dog is only
about 9 inches (23 cm) at the withers,
and the fine silky coat may be either
blue-and-tan or grey/blue-and-tan.
Although it is very small, the Silky
makes a noise which is out of all pro-
portion to its size, and being very possessive of its family and home, makes a
good watchdog.

The YORKSHIRE TERRIER was first
exhibited as a Scotch Terrier at Leeds
in 1861. Much larger than today's
diminutive 'Yorkies' the little broken-
coated dogs had their type fixed by the
addition of the Old English Black-and-

52

Tan Terrier, and, perhaps, of some Maltese to enhance coat quality. Later, size was gradually reduced and by the time it was admitted to the British Kennel Club, in 1886, the Yorkshire Terrier was not only small but very strong and had a luxurious coat. As a show dog, the 'Yorkie' is a dream, repaying careful preparation with a jaunty performance, exhibiting its gloriously long silky coat. It is easy to transport and very economical to keep, but though it looks like a pampered toy, it is a brave, self-assured little dog with personality.

With a close, smooth and glossy coat of the natural black-and-tan pattern found in many old canine breeds, the MANCHESTER TERRIER was known in Britain long before the first dog shows were instituted. The breed was developed from a brown crossbred terrier mated to a Whippet. Their offspring proved excellent for ratting and rabbit coursing, and eventually a strain of black-and-tan terrier evolved which was later called the Manchester Terrier. By 1923 the breed had arrived in the United States and its specialist club was quickly formed. The modern Manchester Terrier weighs in between 12 and 20 lb (5 and 9 kg) and the black-and-tan coat must be smooth, short and glossy. It makes a good pet and house dog, being very clean and well-behaved, is easy to train and likes children.

A toy variety of the Manchester Terrier is recognized by the American Kennel Club where it is known as the MANCHESTER TERRIER (TOY), and is known in England as the English Toy Terrier. Also black-and-tan, it weighs only 6–8 lb (2·5–3·5 kg) and stands about 10 inches (25 cm) high.

Another toy breed with a short close coat and upstanding ears is the MINIATURE PINSCHER, an ancient breed descended from German Terriers. The German Pinscher Club was formed in 1895 but it was not until 1928 that the breed became established in the United States. An excellent house dog although rather reserved with strangers, this compact and elegant little dog with its high-stepping gait may be solid red in colour or black, blue or chocolate with sharply defined tan markings.

The CHIHUAHUA is a very tiny breed which originated in Mexico and is said

to have descended from the sacred dog of the Aztecs. Small, barkless dogs have been recorded in South America for many years, and three black and white puppies were purchased from Mexico in 1888. The American Kennel Club accepted the breed in 1923, and it has since become extremely popular in both Long-coated and Smooth-coated varieties. It makes a superb show dog and a perfect pet. The show Chihuahua should ideally weight between 2 and 4 lb (1 and 2 kg) and may be of any solid or mixed colours.

Usually under 10 inches (25 cm) in height, the quaint little monkey-faced AFFENPINSCHER has an obscure history. It was developed in Germany and was accepted in the United States in 1936. Its coat ideally is black although other

The MINIATURE PINSCHER is a small, neat and very tidy pet, a good watchdog and ideal for town life.

colours are accepted. It is short and dense over most of the body, but is long, loose and shaggy around the eyes, nose and chin. Game and intelligent, the Affenpinscher is very affectionate and makes an appealing little pet.

It is quite likely that the Affenpinscher played a part in the production of another charming toy breed, the GRIFFON BRUXELLOIS. This dog weighs about 8–10 lb (3·5–4·5 kg) and may be bred in the rough-coated variety which is called the Brussels Griffon, or the smooth-coated, variety which is known as the Brabançon. First bred to guard cabs in Brussels, this is a toy with the true terrier spirit. It has remained a fearless little dog and is very possessive about its home and family, so making it an excellent and undemanding watchdog, easily trained, obedient and affectionate. The Brabançon was produced by introducing the smooth coat of the Pug to the original Griffon.

The PUG is a tiny mastiff in type, and so stands alone, because most toys descended from spaniels and terriers. First called the Dutch Pug, its origins are

Above: Here a MINIATURE PINSCHER and his inseparable pal, a SMOOTH-COATED CHIHUAHUA, share their cosy bed.

Right: This AFFENPINSCHER *Late Arrival at Furstin* represents one of the oldest toy breeds of Europe. It is tiny and very rare.

Far right: The GRIFFON BRUXELLOIS is probably descended from the AFFENPINSCHER and other small terriers. This red bitch is *Shandaff Skibbereen Marieta*.

54

obscure, but it is an enchanting little dog with dark, prominent eyes and a tightly curled tail. Its fine soft coat may be either silver, apricot, fawn or black.

Like the Pug, the PEKINGESE has a broad, flat face, but its origins are well-documented and it is known that similar dogs were kept as Royal Dogs in China for several centuries. The Pekingese was first exhibited in England in 1893, and by 1909 the Pekingese Club of America had been formed. This often fierce, strong-willed dog is rewarding to show and the profuse long coat repays expert grooming.

The POMERANIAN is another wonderful show dog and is a miniature Spitz with the typical pointed face and with its tail carried over its back. Only about 4–5 lb (2 kg) in weight, the Pomeranian's profuse stand-off coat may be of any whole colour such as white, black, blue or orange, parti-coloured or shaded-sable. This breed was first shown in the United States in 1900, when white was the most popular colour, but blue and chocolate dogs were also occasionally seen.

The ITALIAN GREYHOUND has also been around for many years but has fluctuated in popularity. A miniaturized version of the Greyhound, this toy breed is finely built but must be sound and stand about 14 inches (35·5 cm) high. Its satin-like coat may be any shade of fawn, white, blue, black, cream, or fawn-and-white pied.

Above: POMERANIANS are very pert and appealing, but despite their small size they enjoy plenty of exercise, fun and family games.

Two small breeds of white dogs are popular. Both have very ancient histories and have been bred down, like the Poodles, from the much larger Water Spaniel or Barbet. The BICHON FRISE and the MALTESE have since followed lines of descent which have produced two quite different, but equally delightful breeds.

The Bichon is sturdy and confident, and its coat, consisting of masses of loose silky curls, is trimmed to give a rounded look to the head and body, and to expose the dark round eyes. About 10 inches (25 cm) high, this agile, gay dog looks very like an animated children's toy.

The Maltese is about the same size as the Bichon but its coat is long, straight and silky. It is easily trained and makes a very loving pet as well as an eye-catching show dog.

Right: The PUG is a unique toy breed, resembling a little MASTIFF. This fine example is *Scarcroft Coppelia.*

Small Spaniels have always been popular as pets, being renowned for their

56

Above: The ITALIAN GREYHOUND is obedient and odourfree, and its satin-like coat needs little grooming.

Left: The glamorous MALTESE TERRIER is the oldest European toy. This is *Pacela Renate of Carmidanick.*

Tueza Taitei is a tiny JAPANESE CHIN, a breed closely related to the PEKINGESE and the PUG.

equable temperament and good house manners.

The ENGLISH TOY SPANIEL, known as the KING CHARLES in Britain, is between 8 and 14 lb (3·6 and 6 kg) in weight and its silky coat may be black-and-tan or ruby, or the broken colours known as Blenheim and Prince Charles. This dog has a short face, large wide-apart eyes and long low-set ears.

The JAPANESE CHIN is more likely to have originated in China, and was probably crossed with King Charles Spaniels

when first introduced to the West at the end of the 19th century. The breed's great character makes it an ideal pet and its profuse silky coat may be either black-and-white or red-and-white.

Tibet has given the Western World several delightfully small dog breeds. The LHASA APSO and the SHIH TZU were first bred in their temples by lamas and were given as special gifts to visiting Chinese dignitaries. These Lion Dogs, as they were then known, were held in great esteem and because they were so

highly prized, were not seen in the Western World until the late 1920s. At first both breeds were classified as one, but eventually two separate standards were approved. Both measure about 10 inches (25 cm) in height and have fine long coats with hair falling over the face. The Lhasa Apso has a straight foreface with a medium stop in the nose, while the Shih Tzu has a short, square muzzle with a pronounced stop. The Shih Tzu can be any colour and is prized for having a white blaze and tail-tip, while the Lhasa Apso may be either golden, sandy, honey, dark grizzle, slate, smoke, parti-colour, black, white or brown. Both are intelligent active little dogs and enjoy the company of their own breed for romping in the garden.

The TIBETAN TERRIER has the same loving temperament of the other breeds from its mountainous homeland, but is a little sharper as befits a true terrier. Standing about 15 inches (38 cm) high, the dog looks very like a miniature sheepdog, with its profuse double coat and long hair falling foward over its large dark eyes. Allowed in any colour except chocolate or liver, the Tibetan Terrier looks attractive when parading in the show ring, and makes an excellent pet and watchdog.

Above: Show-star LHASA APSO dog, Champion *Zhantor Maestro*.

Left: TIBETAN TERRIER *Tingellan Saucy Sue* is typical of this amenable, affectionate and very attractive breed.

59

Caring for Your Dog

Young puppies grow up to be strong and healthy adults when fed the correct diet and allowed to take lots of outdoor exercise.

Much care and thought should be given to the choice of a puppy whether it is to be a pedigree show dog or perhaps a crossbred pet. No animal should ever be bought on impulse, for taking a pet into the home is a serious responsibility and should be treated as such. In choosing the right breed or type of dog you should take several factors into consideration. Active lively breeds need room to exercise freely, long-coated breeds need daily grooming, most wire-haired breeds and terriers need regular expert trimming and poodles must be properly clipped. Some breeds are particularly good with children; some make fearsome guards; some dogs are highly trainable; others, which are naturally independent and wilful, may need more patience and might even need to attend training classes. Family finances should also be considered for the very large breeds, which make very impressive pets, make an equally impressive hole in the weekly household budget. Tiny breeds, on the other hand, generally eat very little – less even than pet cats.

Pedigree puppies should be bought from reputable breeders who may be relied upon to advise to the right choice from the litter and may be contacted after the purchase for hints and help in raising your dog correctly. If you want to show your dog, the breeder will ensure that you choose a puppy with good conformation and a suitable temperament for the ring. If you want a pet, be sure to say so. You may be able to buy a handsome puppy with some minor conformation fault which precludes it from show ring and the price is often adjusted accordingly.

The puppy you choose should be in very good health with bright eyes, a supple, loose-fitting skin and firm feel to its body. There should be no signs of soreness on the skin or around the eyes or nostrils and it should look generally clean and well cared-for. The breeder will give you the young dog's pedigree, showing its recorded ancestry and details of transferring the registration to your ownership. Various vaccination programmes are given to puppies, and

Left: Long-coated puppies should be accustomed to correct grooming from a very early age.

Above: Most puppies learn to get along well with other family pets and enjoy their company.

the relevant certificates will be passed over for your keeping, along with instructions for the continuance of the important veterinary programmes. Puppies are generally wormed, and again, you will be advised on the dates and dosage for further medication. The breeder is the best person to show you how to groom your dog's coat, and will explain the advantages of using certain types of brushes, combs and other grooming aids. Take the trouble to listen carefully at this time for much may be learned from the breeder's long experience and expertise.

Whatever its breed, or type, the young puppy needs normal basic care and spends the first few weeks of life away from its mother just sleeping, eating and growing. It must be carefully and kindly house-broken, too, and this is done by carefully monitoring the little dog's well-defined habits. Most puppies wake from their sleep and after sniffing around for a moment or two, squat down to wet. A little while after eating, puppies empty themselves, and so it is not too difficult to gauge the correct moment to lift your pup and put it firmly onto its litter tray, newspaper, or garden patch reserved for

61

such purposes. Training at this stage must be very simple, and the puppy must be highly praised when it performs well, but never scolded severely when it makes the inevitable and understandable mistakes.

Your new puppy must be given a suitable bed and at this stage a cardboard carton is ideal. Choose one to fit the puppy so that it is able to stretch out comfortably, but is small enough to give a sense of security. You should cut down one side for easy access, put some newspaper in the bottom and an old warm sweater over this for comfort. Small puppies chew everything during their

teething periods so it is pointless to buy smart baskets and bedding at this time. The cartons may be discarded as they are chewed, torn or soiled, and replaced by new ones when necessary. When the dog is adult, it may have its first special bed and cosy cushion.

Correct feeding is important for every dog regardless of its breed, size or age. A puppy is generally given several small meals daily, carefully following the breeder's diet sheet. Then, as it grows, the number of meals decrease, and the quantity increases until the fully mature adult dog is happily able to manage on one substantial daily meal. There are

Right: Always feed your puppy from its own dish. SPANIELS need special bowls to prevent their ears from becoming soiled.

Below: All dogs benefit from training sessions which may be incorporated into periods of play.

62

This little COCKER SPANIEL has been transported to his new home in a safe wicker carrier.

many dog diets and dog owners have their ideas on the best way to feed their dogs. Dogs may be fed fresh raw or cooked meats, and special canine foods are sold in cans, packets and sacks. Most dogs seem to thrive best on the feeding of high quality biscuit and unadulterated fresh or canned meat. Extra-hard biscuits, given as snacks, help to keep the teeth in good condition, and most dogs adore raw-hide bones and toys to chew.

All dogs should be properly trained, learning their names and a few very simple commands from an early age, before progressing to more formal basic training between six and twelve months of age. All training words should be clearly defined, and always used for the same reason. It is important that your dog always comes when it is called, and that it does not jump all over visitors.

Young dogs should be accustomed to travelling in the car. Any sickness symptoms soon disappear if food is withheld for several hours before the journey and the dog regards the trips as treats. It is very important to train your dog not to jump out of the car the minute the door is opened as this behaviour can lead to serious accidents. If fact it is good to teach all dogs to 'wait' in the sitting position while all doors are opened, only passing through when told to 'come'.

63

For regular outings in the car your dog may be prevented from jumping into the passenger seats by fitting a proper guard.

Take advice on choosing the correct collar and lead for your dog. Small dogs need long thin leads, while very tall breeds need short substantial ones. Rolled leather collars look neat and do not mark the hair or skin, but for training a suitable check chain is required. Check chains should be made of thick links as these do not hurt the dog when correctly used, and the chain should be 2 inches (50 mm) longer than the measurement of the dog's neck taken halfway between the head and the body. Check chains should not be left on as normal collars as they might become caught and could strangle your dog. They should only be fitted when a training or lead exercise session is to begin. Dog training schools are wonderful meeting places for dogs and dog owners, and at such classes you are taught how to train your own dog to whatever standard you reuire.

Keep your dog in good health by following a sensible program of regular health checks. Groom your dog properly according to its breed and coat type, and pay particular attention to its ears, teeth and the pads of its feet. Dogs sometimes get very sore pads through treading on hard or sharp stones, and small pebbles may become embedded between the toes. The correct amount and type of exercise for each breed is vitally important and, combined with correct feeding, will produce a dog of which you will be justly proud.

64